REVISE A LEVEL

CW00401547

REVISION PLANNER

Planning your A Level revision: A step-by-step guide

Author: Rob Bircher

Also Available:

REVISE EDEXCEL AS
Mathematics
REVISION GUIDE

REVISE AQA A LEVEL
Psychology
REVISION
GUIDE AND WORKBOOK

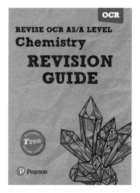

REVISE OCR AS/A LEVEL
Chemistry
REVISION GUIDE

For the full range of Pearson revision titles across KS2, KS3, GCSE, Functional Skills, AS/A Level and BTEC visit:
www.pearsonschools.co.uk/revise

Contents

How to use this book

The aim of this book is to help you prepare for your A Level exams by planning your revision timetable.

Most students find exams stressful: they are important to what you want to do in life, so you want to do well, but they are also challenging with lots to revise. This Planner can help with that. Think of this book as a mini-project to put you in control of your revision. Feeling in control dramatically reduces stress.

The first two parts of this book are a step-by-step guide to planning your revision. Each page will give you something to do or something to find out or think about. The Planner is laid out this way because you need to have a few things sorted before you can put together a really good revision timetable.

Revising for A Level does take time. You will need to plan revision sessions at weekends and in the evenings. It will also take time – a couple of hours – to complete your revision timetable. But this will be time well spent. Your revision will be more **effective** and, because you'll have it all organised, revising will seem **easier** too. You might even find that you have a bit more **spare time**!

Icons used in this book

 = work with your timetable wall chart

 = work with the planner sections in this book

 = write something into this section

 = copy this template to use for different subjects

 = information about how long a section will take

 = check this with your teachers

 = reward yourself with a treat

Worked example = an example of how to fill something in

The revision route

This diagram explains the route that you'll follow in this book.

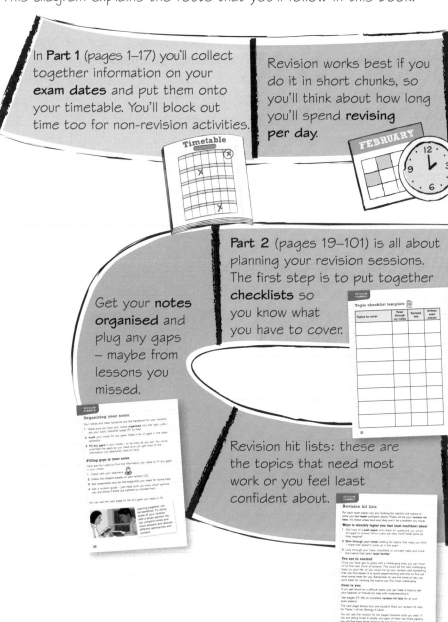

In **Part 1** (pages 1–17) you'll collect together information on your **exam dates** and put them onto your timetable. You'll block out time too for non-revision activities.

Revision works best if you do it in short chunks, so you'll think about how long you'll spend **revising per day.**

Part 2 (pages 19–101) is all about planning your revision sessions. The first step is to put together **checklists** so you know what you have to cover.

Get your **notes organised** and plug any gaps – maybe from lessons you missed.

Revision hit lists: these are the topics that need most work or you feel least confident about.

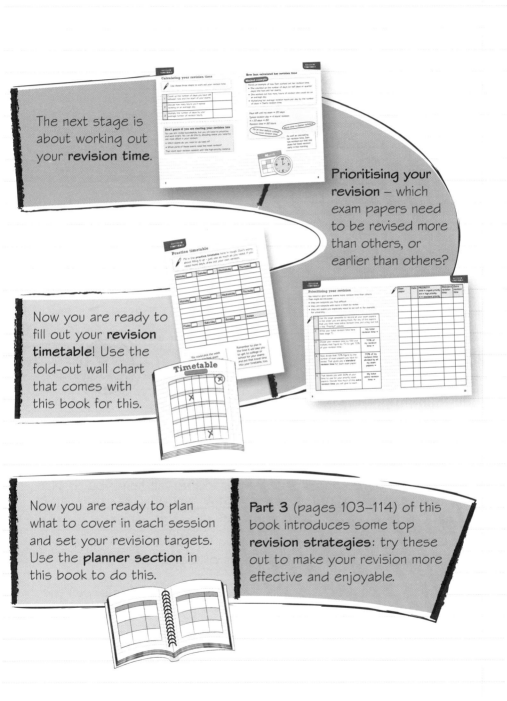

The next stage is about working out your **revision time**.

Prioritising your revision – which exam papers need to be revised more than others, or earlier than others?

Now you are ready to fill out your **revision timetable**! Use the fold-out wall chart that comes with this book for this.

Now you are ready to plan what to cover in each session and set your revision targets. Use the **planner section** in this book to do this.

Part 3 (pages 103–114) of this book introduces some top **revision strategies**: try these out to make your revision more effective and enjoyable.

Part 1: Setting up your revision timetable

Part 1 is about setting up your **revision timetable**. This is the fold-out wall chart that comes with this planner.

When you see the timetable icon, it means you need to do something with your **revision timetable**.

Your revision timetable:

✓ marks out your time for revision

✓ gives you an overview of your revision

✓ gets your revision in the right order.

It should take about 2 hours to work through this section.

Finding out when your exams are

Knowing the dates and times of your exams will help you to plan your **revision timetable**. Some students put all their effort into revising for their first exams. This can leave you under-prepared for later exams. Planning your revision timetable helps make sure you give each exam the right amount of focus.

Your teachers will have all the information about the dates, times and locations of your exams.

It is likely that your exams will not be all in the same place. Make sure you know **where** each exam is going to be, as well as its date and time.

1

Write your exams here in date order: use pencil first. Also include the deadlines for coursework or other non-examination assessments (**NEAs**).

Date / time	Subject and paper	Location (which building/ room)	My target grade
	Exam board and paper code		

Now add the dates to your revision timetable: you could use a red pen or a red sticker so they stand out.

What are your other commitments?

Before you complete your revision timetable, you need to block out time when you know you are already busy.

This could be part-time work, a sports club that you go to every week, a visit away to see a relative, music lessons, band practice – other commitments.

You might need to change some of your commitments if they are right before exams, for example, the evening before an exam.

How do I find out about other commitments?

Are there any family commitments over the revision period that you might not be aware of (or have forgotten about)? These are often recorded on the **family calendar**, if you have one.

There might be some commitments you can skip because you are revising for your exams. But it is good to keep a few things going during your revision time – **especially exercise**. Otherwise you can easily get 'revisioned-out'.

Telling other people about your timetable

Make sure your family knows when you are revising, so they can keep out of your way and let you concentrate.

Do the same for friends so you can **minimise distractions**.

It's a good idea to clear all commitments during the weeks when you are actually taking your exams.

3

Write the other commitments you have during your revision time here.

Commitment	Day and time

 When you are done, block these times out on your **revision timetable**. Use a different coloured pen or highlighter, or stickers, to show that you won't be able to revise during these times.

 Get a family member to check this list and remind you of any commitments you may have missed.

4

What's your study routine?

A routine is when you do the same things at the same times each day. A **revision routine** is a good thing to develop because it helps you **stay on track.**

Some people work best first thing in the morning; others take a while to get started and work best late at night. When do you work best? Use this knowledge to help your routine.

 Use the space below to describe a successful revision day.

- When would it start and finish?

- How long would the revision sessions and breaks be?

- When would you have meals?

- When would your best times for revision be?

- What times of day do you find it hardest to concentrate?

- When would be the best time to build in an exercise session?

- How many hours of revision time are there in total?

Some revision will probably need to take place in the evenings or at weekends. This is a short-term sacrifice for a long-term gain!

Chunking your time

Research shows that we all focus better and feel more motivated when we **break tasks down into chunks**.

For revision this means:

- revising for 20 or 25 minutes, then having a 5-minute break
- varying the topics you are revising.

These things will make your revision more productive. If you also work out when you work best, you can use these chunks for intensive study, perhaps on challenging topic areas. Everyone has times when they find it harder to focus. You can use these less productive chunks of time for routine revision, for example, checking notes or learning lists.

Once you have done two or three chunks, give yourself a longer break – half an hour, for example.

Here's an example of how an A Level student called Chloe chunked a morning of revision time:

10.00–10.25: Business Studies: market mapping

10.25–10.30: break

*10.30–10.55: Business Studies: competitor strengths/
weaknesses*

10.55–11.00: break

11.00–11.30: Biology: Darwin + evolution theory

11.30–12.30: break and lunch! Yoga with Sophie P.

Calculating your revision time

 Use these three steps to work out your revision time.

1	Count up the number of days you have left between now and the start of your exams.	
2	Decide how many hours you'll spend revising on an average day.	
3	Multiply the number of days by your average number of revision hours.	

Don't panic if you are starting your revision late

You can still revise successfully, but you will need to prioritise and work smart. You can do this by deciding where you need to put most effort in your revision:

- Which exams do you need to do best in?
- Which parts of those exams need the most revision?

Then start each revision session with this high-priority material.

7

How Sam calculated her revision time

Worked example

Here's an example of how Sam worked out her revision time.

- She counted up the number of days (or half days or quarter days) she had until her exams.
- She worked out how many hours of revision she could do on an average day.
- Multiplying her average revision hours per day by the number of days = Sam's revision time.

Days left until my exam = 20 days

Typical revision day = 4 hours' revision

4 x 20 days = 80

Revision time = 80 hours

Do an hour before college – my best revision time.

More time in Easter holidays

As well as calculating her revision time, Sam has worked out that she does her best revision early in the morning.

Prioritising your revision

You need to give some exams more revision time than others. That might be because:

- they are subjects you find difficult
- they are subjects with more in them to revise
- they are exams you especially need to do well in, for example, for university.

1	Use the next page to record all your exam papers in the order you are doing them. For any of the papers that you think need extra revision time, put a big red tick in the 'Extra revision time' column.	
2	Write your total revision time here (see page 7).	My total revision time =
3	Divide your revision time by 100 and multiply that figure by 70 to get 70% of your revision time.	70% of my revision time =
4	Now divide that 70% figure by the number of exam papers you have to revise. That gives you a **standard revision time** for each exam paper.	70% of my revision time divided by all my exam papers =
5	That leaves you with 30% of your time to use for your priority exam papers. Decide how much of this **extra revision time** you will give to each.	My total extra revision time =

Exam paper	Date	PRIORITY? *** = urgent priority ** = high priority * = standard priority	Standard revision time	Extra revision time

Filling in your revision timetable

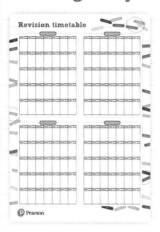

This Revision Planner comes with a fold-out wall chart for you to use as your **revision timetable**.

- Everyone's revision is different. We've left the dates blank so you can fill them in to suit when you start your revision.

- Each day on the revision timetable has a maximum of five revision 'slots'. The lines are faint so you can combine slots together if you want to. Make sure you fill in breaks and free time as well as revision!

- Stickers – people use these in lots of different ways. What works well is using one colour for each subject or each kind of event, for example, exams could be a red or a calming light blue sticker!

What's the point of a revision timetable?

A **revision timetable** can:

✓ help you cover what you need to in the time you have

✓ allow you to prioritise subjects that need more revision

✓ enable you to use your time effectively

✓ spark your motivation to get revising.

Once your **revision timetable** is up on your wall, you just have to follow it – simple!

Getting started

Use the guidelines on the next page to get started.

- You can use the **practice timetable** on pages 13–14 to do your timetable in rough: use a pencil or an erasable pen so you can make revisions.

- Then you can put it together for real on the actual **revision timetable**

Revision timetable guidelines

1 What should be on your timetable already?

   a All your exams – check you've got them on the right days.

   b All your other commitments – block that time out.

2 You know what your revision time is for each paper – now you can slot that time into your revision timetable.

   a Start with a priority exam paper – one that needs extra revision time or has exams early (see page 10).

   b Work backwards from the day of the first exam. You will want to spend half a day (or more) revising that paper either the morning before the exam (if it is in the afternoon) or the day before – so block out that time now.

   c Now 'spend' the rest of your revision time for that paper, putting in a chunk here and there as you work backwards through the timetable, until all the time is spent.

   d Do the same thing for all the top priority/early papers.

   e Then move on to the rest of the exam papers until all your revision time is used up.

It is a good idea to vary your revision chunks so you cover different subjects through the day.

Try scheduling your toughest subjects so they come first in the day. That way you'll be tackling them when you are fresh.

Revision timetable

Practice timetable

Fill in the **practice timetable** here in rough. Don't worry about filling it up – just use as much as you need. If you need more days, draw out your own version.

Monday		Tuesday		Wednesday		Thursday	
Monday		**Tuesday**		**Wednesday**		**Thursday**	
Monday		**Tuesday**		**Wednesday**		**Thursday**	

You could pick the week before your first exam and the week of your first exam for this practice.

Remember to plan in the time it will take you to get to college or school for your exams and put that travel time into your timetable, too.

When you have finished, fill in your real **revision timetable** using your fold-out wall chart. Use a pencil or an erasable pen – revision plans can change.

Friday	Saturday	Sunday	Notes

Friday	Saturday	Sunday	Notes

Friday	Saturday	Sunday	Notes

On the day before your first exam, you will probably want to spend a significant amount of time revising for that exam.

You have worked out how much time you have to spend revising for each exam paper on page 10. Use those totals to plan your revision.

Include other commitments in your revision timetable (see page 4).

Rewards

Staying motivated is really important. A good way to stay motivated in your revision is to:

1 set yourself **targets**

2 **reward** yourself when you hit your targets.

Setting targets

It's a good idea to set a **target** before each chunk of revision. For example: to complete a topic, to condense three pages of notes or to answer an exam question under timed conditions.

Remember to make your targets achievable and realistic.

Planning rewards

Reward yourself when you hit your targets. You'll need to think about what rewards would work best for you. Some ideas might be:

- **Small rewards** for hitting a revision target, e.g. a 5-minute break, a chunk of chocolate, listen to a favourite song.
- **Medium rewards** for completing all your targets for a day or for the week, or after each exam, e.g. a cinema visit, a gaming session, a night out with friends.
- **Large rewards** once all your exams are over, e.g. a holiday break or time out with friends.

Planning your rewards

 Plan some realistic **targets** and **rewards** here.

My target	My reward
Small	
Medium	
Large	

Your first **reward** should be for completing your **revision timetable**.

What will your reward be?

Reviewing your revision

You might not feel like you have time to think about your revision as well as doing it, but research shows that taking a little time each day to review your revision really **helps you remember more.**

- Start each revision day with a 5-minute session thinking about what you want to achieve that day.
- Spend 5 minutes at the end of your revision for the day reviewing what you have done.
- Make a list of what you plan to cover next.

Reviewing your revision timetable

Now you have finished Part 1 and have completed your revision timetable.

Take a few minutes now to review your timetable.

- Fix any little mistakes or problems with it.
- Research says it is a good idea to think about challenges ahead, as this helps you deal with them. So if there are some tough-looking days ahead, face up to them and think of ways to tackle them.
- Taking the time to complete Part 1 is an important achievement. You have taken control of your revision, which also means getting a grip on exam stress.

> Experts agree that students who have a revision timetable (and stick to it) usually do better in their exams than students who do not.

Space for reflection

Use this space to record your thoughts on your revision.

- the challenges so far
- the challenges ahead
- the ways you are going to tackle the challenges.

'A stumbling block can also be a stepping stone.'
This means that facing up to a challenge often turns out to be just what you needed to get on track to success.

Part 2: Planning your revision sessions

What do you need to revise?

Part 2 is about planning your revision sessions. You'll do this in the **planner**: the section of this book that looks like a diary (pages 61–100).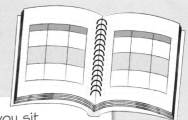

A revision session is the time when you sit down to do several chunks of revision.
It is **important to plan** them so that you:
✓ cover everything you need for each paper
✓ know what to revise each day
✓ stay focused on your targets for each session.

It should take about 2 hours to work through this part (if you already have topic lists for your exams), plus about 30 minutes a week planning your revision sessions.

Each exam paper you do has a list of topics and/or skills to cover. You can find these topics and skills listed in the **specification** for each subject. Check this with your teacher or tutor.

You can use the lists of topics and/or skills to **put together a checklist** for each exam you are doing. There's an example opposite on page 20. There's a blank one that you can copy as many times as you need to on page 21.

Most A Level subjects contain different options: often each paper will involve option choices. As well as knowing your exam board and specification, make sure you are sure which options you did in class. That way you won't end up revising more topics than you need to!

Worked example

History Paper 2 (depth study) option 2C.2 Russia in revolution, 1894–1924

Topics to cover	Read through my notes	Revised this	Written exam answer
The rule of Nicholas II, 1894–1905 The nature of autocratic rule: • the Tsarist principles of autocracy, nationality and orthodoxy • the oppression of nationalities • the Okhrana	✓	✓	✓
Opposition to Tsarism: • unrest among peasants and workers • middle-class opposition and the League of Liberation • the Socialist Revolutionaries and the Social Democrats • reasons for the lack of success of opposition groups	✓	✓	
The 1905 Revolution: • the impact of the Russo-Japanese war • Bloody Sunday • the spread of revolutionary activity among peasants, workers and national minorities • the St. Petersburg Soviet			
Nicholas II's response: • the failure of the August Manifesto • the October Manifesto and the response of opposition groups • the crushing of the Moscow Uprising • the extent of the recovery of Tsarist power	✓	✓	✓
The end of Romanov rule, 1906–17 Change and continuity in government: • the Fundamental Law • the radicalism of the first two dumas • Nicholas II's relations with the dumas, 1906–14 • the nature of Tsarist government and royal power in 1914			

Topic checklist template

Topics to cover	Read through my notes	Revised this	Written exam answer

Topic checklist – concept map

Some subjects have clear-cut sections, but others can seem more complicated, with topics connecting in different ways.

For these subjects, it may be easier to present your checklist as a **concept map**. You can find out more about making **concept maps** on page 107. Here's an example of one topic of an AS and A Level Psychology course.

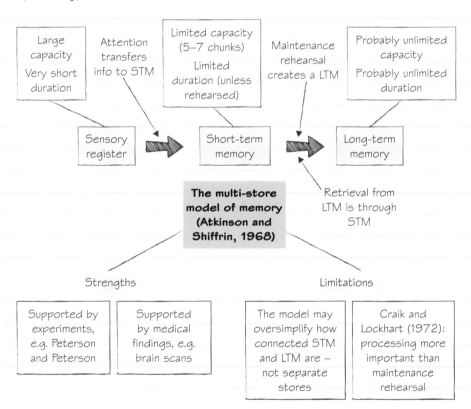

Large capacity
Very short duration

Attention transfers info to STM

Limited capacity (5–7 chunks)
Limited duration (unless rehearsed)

Maintenance rehearsal creates a LTM

Probably unlimited capacity
Probably unlimited duration

Sensory register

Short-term memory

Long-term memory

The multi-store model of memory (Atkinson and Shiffrin, 1968)

Retrieval from LTM is through STM

Strengths

Limitations

Supported by experiments, e.g. Peterson and Peterson

Supported by medical findings, e.g. brain scans

The model may oversimplify how connected STM and LTM are – not separate stores

Craik and Lockhart (1972): processing more important than maintenance rehearsal

Organising your notes

Your notes and class handouts are the backbone for your revision.

1 Make sure you have your notes **organised** into the right units — use your topic checklist (page 21) to help.

2 **Audit** your notes for any gaps. Make a list of gaps in the table opposite.

3 **Fill any gaps** in your notes — or as many as you can. You could prioritise the gaps so you make sure you get hold of the information you absolutely have to have.

Filling gaps in your notes

Here are four ways to find the information you need to fill any gaps in your notes.

1 Check with your teachers.

2 Check the subject pages on your school VLE.

3 Ask classmates who do the subject(s) you need for some help.

4 Get a revision guide — just make sure you know which options you are doing if there are options to choose from.

You can use the next page to list any gaps you need to fill.

Learning together can be beneficial. Try doing some of your revision with a study partner. You can compare notes and mock answers and discuss different approaches and content.

Gaps in my notes that I need to fill

Subject/topic	Missing notes – description	PRIORITY

Revision hit lists

For each exam paper you are revising for, identify the topics or skills you feel **least** confident about. These will be your **revision hit lists**: hit these areas hard and they won't be a problem any more!

Ways to identify topics you feel least confident about

1 Get hold of a **past paper** and check for questions you would struggle to answer. Which topic are they from? What skills do they require?

2 **Skim through your notes** looking for topics that make you think: 'I hope that doesn't come up in the exam'.

3 Look through your topic checklists or concept maps and circle the topics that seem **least familiar**.

You are in control!

Once you have got to grips with a challenging area, you can move on to the next chunk of revision. This could be the next challenging topic on your list, or you could mix up your revision with something that you find easier. It is worth experimenting with this to find out what works best for you. Remember to use the times of day you work best for revising the topics you find most challenging.

Over to you

If you get stuck on a difficult topic, you can make a note to ask your teacher or friends for help with understanding it.

Use pages 27–56 to complete **revision hit lists** for all your exam papers.

The next page shows how one student filled out revision hit lists for Paper 1 of her Biology A Level.

You can use the revision hit list pages however suits you best. If you are doing three A Levels, and each of them has three papers, you will find here three revision hit list pages per paper: enough to get your revision started.

Worked example

Here's an example of how to use the **revision hit lists**.

Revision hit list

Subject: Biology   **Exam paper**: Advanced Biochemistry, Microbiology and Genetics

Topic	Where to start
Modern Genetics	Factors affecting gene expression: understanding epigenetic modification
Energy for Biological Processes	I need to learn the processes in glycolysis.
Exchange and Transport	Maths skills: linear relationships, rate of change. Calculating surface areas is OK.

Topic	Where to start
Microbiology and Pathogens	Learn the different measuring methods (including dilution plating).
Classification and Biodiversity	Classification: difficulties and limitations of species definition (missed this lesson)
Classification and Biodiversity	Calculating the index of diversity
Biological Molecules	The practical on rates of enzyme-controlled reactions
Cells, Viruses and Reproduction	Functions of organelles: the 12 key ones I need to learn

Revision hit list

Subject: Exam paper:

Topic	Where to start

Topic	Where to start

Topic	Where to start

Revision hit list

Subject: Exam paper:

Topic	Where to start

Topic	Where to start

Topic	Where to start

Revision hit list

Subject: Exam paper:

Topic	Where to start

Topic	Where to start

Topic	Where to start

Revision hit list

Subject: Exam paper:

Topic	Where to start

Topic	Where to start

Topic	Where to start

Revision hit list

Subject: Exam paper:

Topic	Where to start

Topic	Where to start

Topic	Where to start

Revision hit list

Subject: Exam paper:

Topic	Where to start

Topic	Where to start

Topic	Where to start

Revision hit list

Subject: Exam paper:

Topic	Where to start

Topic	Where to start

Topic	Where to start

Revision hit list

Subject: Exam paper:

Topic	Where to start

Topic	Where to start

Topic	Where to start

Revision hit list

Subject: Exam paper:

Topic	Where to start

Topic	Where to start

Topic	Where to start

Revision hit list

Subject: Exam paper:

Topic	Where to start

Topic	Where to start

Topic	Where to start

Revision hit list

Subject: Exam paper:

Topic	Where to start

Topic	Where to start

Topic	Where to start

Revision hit list

Subject: Exam paper:

Topic	Where to start

Topic	Where to start

Topic	Where to start

Revision hit list

Subject: Exam paper:

Topic	Where to start

Topic	Where to start

Topic	Where to start

Revision hit list

Subject: Exam paper:

Topic	Where to start

Topic	Where to start

Topic	Where to start

Revision hit list

Subject: Exam paper:

Topic	Where to start

Topic	Where to start

Topic	Where to start

Revision hit list

Subject: Exam paper:

Topic	Where to start

Topic	Where to start

Topic	Where to start

Revision hit list

Subject: Exam paper:

Topic	Where to start

Topic	Where to start

Topic	Where to start

Revision hit list

Subject: Exam paper:

Topic	Where to start

Topic	Where to start

Topic	Where to start

Revision hit list

Subject: Exam paper:

Topic	Where to start

Topic	Where to start

Topic	Where to start

Revision hit list

Subject: Exam paper:

Topic	Where to start

Topic	Where to start

Topic	Where to start

Revision hit list

Subject: Exam paper:

Topic	Where to start

Topic	Where to start

Topic	Where to start

Revision hit list

Subject: Exam paper:

Topic	Where to start

Topic	Where to start

Topic	Where to start

Revision hit list

Subject: Exam paper:

Topic	Where to start

Topic	Where to start

Topic	Where to start

Revision hit list

Subject: Exam paper:

Topic	Where to start

Topic	Where to start

Topic	Where to start

Revision hit list

Subject: Exam paper:

Topic	Where to start

Topic	Where to start

Topic	Where to start

Revision hit list

Subject: Exam paper:

Topic	Where to start

Topic	Where to start

Topic	Where to start

Revision hit list

Subject: Exam paper:

Topic	Where to start

Topic	Where to start

Topic	Where to start

53

Revision hit list

Subject: Exam paper:

Topic	Where to start

Topic	Where to start

Topic	Where to start

Revision hit list

Subject: Exam paper:

Topic	Where to start

Topic	Where to start

Topic	Where to start

Revision hit list

Subject: Exam paper:

Topic	Where to start

Topic	Where to start

Topic	Where to start

Setting revision session targets

A **revision session** is the time when you sit down to do **several chunks of revision**. You need short breaks between the chunks, and longer breaks between sessions.

Why should I set session targets?

If you **decide what you want to achieve** in each revision session, your revision will be more effective and you will feel more motivated.

When should I set my session targets?

It's up to you when you **decide what your targets are** for each session: it might be just before you start the session, or it might be something you plan for a day or a week.

What should my targets be?

This is up to you, too! Here are some ideas:

- Your revision hit lists are a good place to start. You could decide to tackle one challenging area at the start of each session.

- You could have the target of answering a practice exam question in your session.

- You could have the target of avoiding distractions: for example, not checking your phone until a break between revision chunks.

- You could have the target of writing against the clock: giving yourself a set time to write an answer to an exam question. Knowing how much you can write in a set time is a very valuable exam skill.

Here are some tips on setting targets:

✓ Make your targets **time-specific**: decide how long you will give yourself to achieve them.

✓ Your targets should be **realistic**.

✓ Make sure your targets are **useful** for your revision.

✓ If you use the same targets each session, they could become boring. Throw in some **variety** – even some unusual targets once in a while! (But still useful, of course.)

✓ **Reward** yourself for achieving your targets!

 Use this space to record different ideas for revision session targets.

Using the revision planner

 Now you are ready to use all the information you've put together to start planning your revision sessions. You will use the **planner** section of this book (pages 61–100) for this.

Important: We've included plenty of **planner** pages, which may be more than you need. You can use these pages to plan revision for mock exams, too.

What's the point of planning revision sessions?

You know from your revision timetable what exam papers you are revising for each day, so why do you need to plan each session too? Planning what you will do in each revision session is useful because it helps you:

1 cover everything you need for each paper – starting with the problem areas!

2 know what topics to revise each day

3 stay focused on your targets for each session.

> Many people find it easier to plan their revision sessions for a week at a time. This gives you more flexibility than planning for months in advance.

What is the difference between your timetable and the planner?

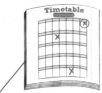

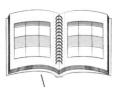

What exam papers you are revising for each day.

Details of what you are going to revise in each session.

Getting started

Here are some tips on using the **planner** section to plan your revision sessions.

The **planner** section has spaces for five revision sessions in a day. You can use as many or as few of these as you have time for.

Make a note of your **rewards** here: for finishing a whole week, a whole day, a session and/or a chunk – it's up to you.

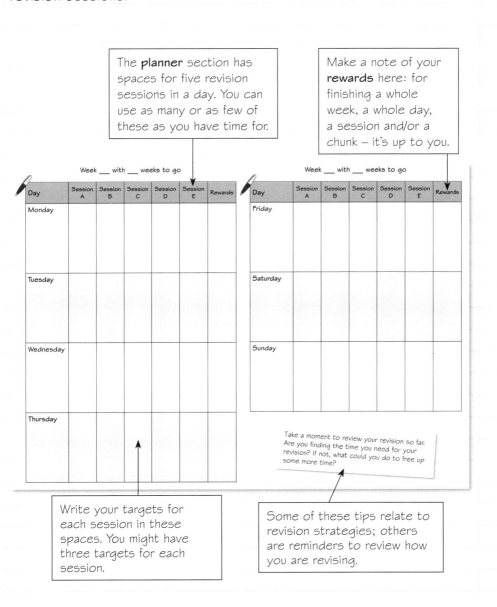

Week ___ with ___ weeks to go						
Day	Session A	Session B	Session C	Session D	Session E	Rewards
Monday						
Tuesday						
Wednesday						
Thursday						

Week ___ with ___ weeks to go						
Day	Session A	Session B	Session C	Session D	Session E	Rewards
Friday						
Saturday						
Sunday						

Take a moment to review your revision so far. Are you finding the time you need for your revision? If not, what could you do to free up some more time?

Write your targets for each session in these spaces. You might have three targets for each session.

Some of these tips relate to revision strategies; others are reminders to review how you are revising.

Week ___ with ___ weeks to go

Day	Session A	Session B	Session C	Session D	Session E	Rewards
Monday						
Tuesday						
Wednesday						
Thursday						

Week ___ with ___ weeks to go

Day	Session A	Session B	Session C	Session D	Session E	Rewards
Friday						
Saturday						
Sunday						

Keep yourself motivated with a reward when you hit your revision targets.

Week ___ with ___ weeks to go

Day	Session A	Session B	Session C	Session D	Session E	Rewards
Monday						
Tuesday						
Wednesday						
Thursday						

Week ___ with ___ weeks to go

Day	Session A	Session B	Session C	Session D	Session E	Rewards
Friday						
Saturday						
Sunday						

Take a moment to review your revision so far.
Are you finding the time you need for your
revision? If not, what could you do to free up
some more time?

Week ___ with ___ weeks to go

Day	Session A	Session B	Session C	Session D	Session E	Rewards
Monday						
Tuesday						
Wednesday						
Thursday						

Week ___ with ___ weeks to go

Day	Session A	Session B	Session C	Session D	Session E	Rewards
Friday						
Saturday						
Sunday						

Take the time you need to read exam questions very carefully. Make sure you know exactly what each exam question is asking you to do before you start writing your answer.

Week ___ with ___ weeks to go

Day	Session A	Session B	Session C	Session D	Session E	Rewards
Monday						
Tuesday						
Wednesday						
Thursday						

Week ___ with ___ weeks to go

Day	Session A	Session B	Session C	Session D	Session E	Rewards
Friday						
Saturday						
Sunday						

Think about the way you've been revising.
Which strategies have worked well for you?
How could you improve them even further?

Week ___ with ___ weeks to go

Day	Session A	Session B	Session C	Session D	Session E	Rewards
Monday						
Tuesday						
Wednesday						
Thursday						

Week ___ with ___ weeks to go

Day	Session A	Session B	Session C	Session D	Session E	Rewards
Friday						
Saturday						
Sunday						

One of the best ways to revise for an exam is to practise answering questions from previous papers. Ask your teachers to help you find good questions to practise.

Week ___ with ___ weeks to go

Day	Session A	Session B	Session C	Session D	Session E	Rewards
Monday						
Tuesday						
Wednesday						
Thursday						

Week ___ with ___ weeks to go

Day	Session A	Session B	Session C	Session D	Session E	Rewards
Friday						
Saturday						
Sunday						

A Level exams are often 'bunched' together rather than being spread out. This can make revising for the 'bunch' of papers more challenging: another good reason for planning your revision time carefully. You can keep revising in between exams, but remember to get plenty of rest too, as having lots of exams is very tiring.

Week ___ with ___ weeks to go

Day	Session A	Session B	Session C	Session D	Session E	Rewards
Monday						
Tuesday						
Wednesday						
Thursday						

Week ___ with ___ weeks to go

Day	Session A	Session B	Session C	Session D	Session E	Rewards
Friday						
Saturday						
Sunday						

If you used the revision hit list idea on pages 27–56 of this book, then don't forget to keep coming back to those tricky topic areas in your revision.

Week ___ with ___ weeks to go

Day	Session A	Session B	Session C	Session D	Session E	Rewards
Monday						
Tuesday						
Wednesday						
Thursday						

Week ___ with ___ weeks to go

Day	Session A	Session B	Session C	Session D	Session E	Rewards
Friday						
Saturday						
Sunday						

If you hit areas of your revision that you don't understand fully, make a note of them and discuss them with your teacher or tutor.

Week ___ with ___ weeks to go

Day	Session A	Session B	Session C	Session D	Session E	Rewards
Monday						
Tuesday						
Wednesday						
Thursday						

Week ___ with ___ weeks to go

Day	Session A	Session B	Session C	Session D	Session E	Rewards
Friday						
Saturday						
Sunday						

It's important to review your revision as you go along. What sorts of revision techniques are working best? How far are you through your topic checklists? You can always update your revision timetable to pick up some pace if you have missed revision sessions.

Week ___ with ___ weeks to go

Day	Session A	Session B	Session C	Session D	Session E	Rewards
Monday						
Tuesday						
Wednesday						
Thursday						

Week ___ with ___ weeks to go

Day	Session A	Session B	Session C	Session D	Session E	Rewards
Friday						
Saturday						
Sunday						

What are the three biggest distractions you are finding in your revision? How could you turn those into rewards for getting a revision session completed?

Week ___ with ___ weeks to go

Day	Session A	Session B	Session C	Session D	Session E	Rewards
Monday						
Tuesday						
Wednesday						
Thursday						

Week ___ with ___ weeks to go

Day	Session A	Session B	Session C	Session D	Session E	Rewards
Friday						
Saturday						
Sunday						

It's a good idea to start your revision day with a topic you find challenging. You'll feel a sense of achievement and you may be able to remember more when your brain is fresh.

Week ___ with ___ weeks to go

Day	Session A	Session B	Session C	Session D	Session E	Rewards
Monday						
Tuesday						
Wednesday						
Thursday						

Week ___ with ___ weeks to go

Day	Session A	Session B	Session C	Session D	Session E	Rewards
Friday						
Saturday						
Sunday						

It is a good idea to revise in chunks of time: around 20–25 minutes per chunk. Try not to get distracted. Focus on your revision, then have a 5-minute break before the next chunk.

Week ___ with ___ weeks to go

Day	Session A	Session B	Session C	Session D	Session E	Rewards
Monday						
Tuesday						
Wednesday						
Thursday						

Week ___ with ___ weeks to go

Day	Session A	Session B	Session C	Session D	Session E	Rewards
Friday						
Saturday						
Sunday						

Just reading and re-reading your notes is not the best way to revise. Use memory strategies to process information into something you find easy to remember. See page 105 for help with this.

Week ___ with ___ weeks to go

Day	Session A	Session B	Session C	Session D	Session E	Rewards
Monday						
Tuesday						
Wednesday						
Thursday						

Week ___ with ___ weeks to go

Day	Session A	Session B	Session C	Session D	Session E	Rewards
Friday						
Saturday						
Sunday						

Did you know that occasionally eating a little bit of dark chocolate is supposed to give your brain a mini-power boost? Try it and see if it works for you.

Week ___ with ___ weeks to go

Day	Session A	Session B	Session C	Session D	Session E	Rewards
Monday						
Tuesday						
Wednesday						
Thursday						

Week ___ with ___ weeks to go

Day	Session A	Session B	Session C	Session D	Session E	Rewards
Friday						
Saturday						
Sunday						

If you need to remember examples or case studies for your exam, practise using relevant information from your examples to answer the different sorts of questions.

Week ___ with ___ weeks to go

Day	Session A	Session B	Session C	Session D	Session E	Rewards
Monday						
Tuesday						
Wednesday						
Thursday						

Week ___ with ___ weeks to go

Day	Session A	Session B	Session C	Session D	Session E	Rewards
Friday						
Saturday						
Sunday						

Spending a short amount of time at the end of each day to quickly review what you've covered can work really well. You can also start each day's revision by recapping what you did the previous day.

Week ___ with ___ weeks to go

Day	Session A	Session B	Session C	Session D	Session E	Rewards
Monday						
Tuesday						
Wednesday						
Thursday						

Week ___ with ___ weeks to go

Day	Session A	Session B	Session C	Session D	Session E	Rewards
Friday						
Saturday						
Sunday						

Use the timer on your phone to make sure you keep to time targets – but switch off other notifications to avoid distractions as you revise.

REVISION PLANNER

Week ___ with ___ weeks to go

Day	Session A	Session B	Session C	Session D	Session E	Rewards
Monday						
Tuesday						
Wednesday						
Thursday						

95

Week ___ with ___ weeks to go

Day	Session A	Session B	Session C	Session D	Session E	Rewards
Friday						
Saturday						
Sunday						

How many days in a row can you meet your revision targets? A 5-day streak should be worth a pretty good reward!

Week ___ with ___ weeks to go

Day	Session A	Session B	Session C	Session D	Session E	Rewards
Monday						
Tuesday						
Wednesday						
Thursday						

Week ___ with ___ weeks to go

Day	Session A	Session B	Session C	Session D	Session E	Rewards
Friday						
Saturday						
Sunday						

Revision classes at college or school are excellent, but they are not a substitute for revising on your own — unless you are the only one in the class answering all the teacher's questions.

Week ___ with ___ weeks to go

Day	Session A	Session B	Session C	Session D	Session E	Rewards
Monday						
Tuesday						
Wednesday						
Thursday						

Week ___ with ___ weeks to go

Day	Session A	Session B	Session C	Session D	Session E	Rewards
Friday						
Saturday						
Sunday						

There is a day in your future, sometime in August, when you will get your A Level grades. What do you want to see on that day? Use this picture to motivate your revision.

Reviewing your revision

You have reached the end of Part 2. In the same way as you reviewed your revision timetable at the end of Part 1, you should now review your Revision Planner.

✓ Look quickly through your revision checklists and hit lists.

✓ Reflect on how organised you are now for your revision, and how much this will help you do well – which it really will!

✓ Think ahead to challenging topics and days when it might be hard to get motivated. Consider some tactics you could use to help you keep going.

Making time to review your revision as you start and finish each session is a very effective revision technique. Here are some questions you could use to focus your 5-minute reviews:

? What do I know now that I didn't know (or remember) at the start of the session?

? How does what I've revised today link to what I've already covered for this subject?

? Based on what I've revised today, what do I think I should revise next?

? Thinking about the way I revise, what strategies worked best for me?

? Is there anything I could change about the way I revise to make it more effective?

? How would I summarise what I've covered this session in five points?

Space for reflection

 Use this space to record your thoughts on your revision:

- the challenges so far
- the challenges ahead
- how you'll tackle the challenges.

Part 3: Revision strategies

Part 3 gives you a quick guide to some tried-and-tested revision strategies.

Revision strategies make your revision:

✓ more effective (you learn more and learn better)
✓ more varied (less boring)
✓ easier and quicker.

It should take about 30 minutes to read through this section. Remember to come back to this section for ideas on making your revision really work for you.

Understanding revision

The way most of us tend to revise is to read through things several times and hope some of the information sticks. In fact, this isn't the best way to revise. You need to **unpick the information** and then explain it to yourself.

This is because your brain learns best when you ask it to make **connections and create meanings**.

Making revision work for you

Not all these revision strategies will work for you, and some will be better for some subjects than others. If you get stuck with revising a topic in one way, try out another strategy to see if that helps.

To test out a revision strategy, try it and then test how much you remember a) immediately after the revision and then b) the next day.

If you've been successful in making connections and creating your own meanings in your revision, then it is much more likely that you will have succeeded in moving information to long-term memory. Your long-term memory is what you'll rely on in your exams.

Condensing your notes

Condensing your notes means making **summaries of the main points**. Why is this a good idea?

✓ Making the summaries is good revision.

✓ The summaries are a lot easier to revise from.

There are **four steps** to condensing your notes:

1 Get your notes organised (see page 23).

2 For each page of your notes, write a summary of the main points on a piece of paper.

3 Condense each summary down to the main ideas, key terms and key points.

4 Write your condensed notes on index cards, leaving plenty of space between points.

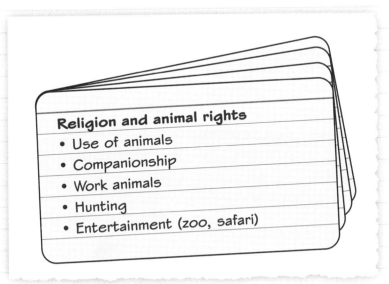

Religion and animal rights
- Use of animals
- Companionship
- Work animals
- Hunting
- Entertainment (zoo, safari)

Condensing notes helps you use them as memory triggers for recalling the details of a topic, its key issues and the evidence that you will need to answer fully in your exam.

Memory strategies

Memory strategies are **tried-and-tested ways of helping your brain remember things**. There are lots of different methods. Here are three of the best:

Mnemonics

Use the first letters of a list of things you need to remember to make up a **memorable phrase**.

For example, here are six types of hard-engineering coastal defences: **r**ip-rap, **s**ea walls, **r**evetments, **o**ffshore reefs, **g**roynes, **g**abions. The first letters could make up the phrase: *Rip Saws Really Open Great Gaps*.

Putting things in your own words

Read your notes, then turn the page over and see how much of the information you can write down.

Now read your notes again. Then **explain what they mean to someone else**, or just out loud to yourself. Turn your notes over and see how much you can recall this time. It should be more.

Make unusual connections

Your brain locks on to things that seem unusual. Try thinking of **weird connections** to things you need to remember. For example, if you had to remember that Patrick Manson discovered the spread of disease by mosquitoes, you could imagine a man and his son running from a huge mosquito.

Flashcards

Flashcards are often used in Languages because they are great for testing yourself on vocabulary. You could use them for testing yourself on key terms in lots of other subjects, too.

Flashcards have something to remember on one side of a card, and the explanation or definition on the other; you can make them using card or paper. It can also be useful to make a presentation with the first slide of a pair being the thing you need to revise, and the next slide being the answer.

Successful revision strategy sequence

Combine approaches for a **revision 'power-up'**:

✓ Condense your notes.

✓ Explain your summaries to someone else.

✓ Make flashcards from your summary points.

✓ Test yourself using your flashcards.

A lot of people use highlighter pens to identify things they need to remember in their notes. This doesn't really engage your brain in making connections so it isn't always a very effective way of revising.

106

Getting visual

Drawing diagrams and using pictures can be a powerful way to process information and make it more memorable.

Flow charts

These are good for revising **processes**. For example, the life of a product in Product Design:

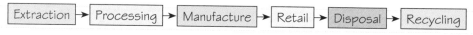

Extraction → Processing → Manufacture → Retail → Disposal → Recycling

Concept maps

Concept maps are a good way of revising **how one thing connects to something else**. A good technique is to start one as you start revising a new topic and map the connections as you go through. Once it is done, hide it and try to redraw it.

Tips for good concept maps

1 Use a **big piece of paper** – A3 size; or do your map on-screen so you've plenty of room to expand.

2 Use **different colours** for the different branches of your map.

3 Use **pictures** (unusual ones if possible) in your map to help you remember it.

See page 22 for more on concept maps.

107

Past papers and mark schemes

Past papers are **old exam papers**. Mark schemes are guidelines on what marks examiners should give for different kinds of answers.

Why use past papers for revision?

Trying out older versions of the exams you will be sitting is excellent practice because:

- you get to know how your exam papers work
- you get a chance to try out what you know with real questions
- you can find out how to improve your answers
- you get to understand what your examiners are looking for.

How do mark schemes work?

Mark schemes can be very simple for some questions – they give the right answer or answers. For longer questions they are trickier though: ask your teacher for help.

Where can I find past papers and mark schemes?

On your exam board's websites, but because exams change quite often, it is best to ask your teachers for past papers and mark schemes so you use the right ones for your courses.

Understanding exam questions

There are lots of different types of exam question, but there are three main steps to answering all of them.

1 Read the question **very carefully.**

2 Underline the **command term(s).**

3 Use the **marks** available to **plan** your answer.

What are command terms?

These are words in the question that tell you what to do. Here are some common ones and what they mean.

Outline	Give the key points but don't go into detail.
Describe	Give a detailed account of something.
Explain	Set out a detailed account that includes reasons and results; causes and effects.
Compare	Identify the similarities and differences between things in a balanced way.
Evaluate	Work out the value of something by weighing up its strengths and its limitations.

How do I plan my answer?

The marks for the question will show you roughly how many points to make (roughly 1 per mark) and how long to spend on it (roughly 1 minute per mark). That is a **rough** guide!

When you are practising writing exam answers against the clock, use the 'mark a minute' guidance to set the time limit you are writing to.

Usually, the questions that are worth the most marks on an exam paper involve **extended answers** – that means answers where you have to write quite a lot to explain your thinking.

Here are three more tips for dealing with extended answer questions.

4 Keep your answer **relevant** to the question.

5 **Connect** your points together with linking terms.

6 Use **paragraphs** to help to give your answer a clear structure.

Stay relevant

Every point you make should be **answering the question**. This is why it is so important to make sure you really understand what the question is asking, rather than plunging in and writing whatever you can remember about the topic. Keep referring back to the question throughout your answer.

Linking terms

Some exam answers are a mess of points all tangled together. You can avoid this by using links like 'Another reason is...' or 'However...' They signpost where your argument is going.

Bloom's taxonomy

Behind a lot of what happens in education is
a theory about different stages of learning
known as **Bloom's taxonomy**. (A taxonomy is
a way of classifying something.) It is named
after a psychologist called Benjamin
Bloom, who was part of a movement in
US education to add more challenge
to students' learning in school.

Bloom's taxonomy is often
summarised in a pyramid-shaped
diagram like this one:

Creating

Evaluating

Analysing

Applying

Understanding

Remembering

Bloom's taxonomy and exam questions

At the bottom of the pyramid are the simplest type of learning
activities, which are about remembering facts. We often start
lessons by seeing how much we can remember about the topic.
Each level up the pyramid is then a step up in complexity, until you
get to the top where tasks require a lot of high-level thinking skills.

Exam questions have a strong connection to Bloom's taxonomy. The
highest mark questions tend to involve high-level thinking skills such
as evaluation. The lowest mark questions are likely to be knowledge
recall. For example, a question that asks 'What is the bottom level
of Bloom's taxonomy?' is about remembering. A question that asks
'Evaluate the importance of Bloom's taxonomy in education today'
will require high-level thinking skills.

You can use Bloom's taxonomy in your revision. As well as
seeing how much you can remember from your notes, practise
applying your knowledge using past papers. For a real challenge,
try creating your own exam questions and then answering them!

Top exam tips

Here are some top exam tips from students who did well in their A Levels:

If you can, start your revision as early as possible. You need time to go over topics two or three times.

Get plenty of sleep the night before an exam.

Get lots of past papers, and work through them and use the mark schemes to see what you got right and what you could have done better.

If you've got big exams at the start of your exam time, then don't just revise for them. You need to do revision for the later exams, too.

I put sticky notes with key words on them all round the house so everywhere I went I was revising!

Don't be frightened to ask your teachers for help – they'll be really glad to help you all they can.

The Easter holidays are your prime revision time: make sure you use that time to get serious about your revision.

Be prepared – exam day reminders

✓ Make sure you know **when** and **where** your exam is taking place.

✓ Aim to get to school **at least 15 minutes before** your exam starts, in case of any transport problems. There will be a seating plan to show you where you are sitting in the exam room or hall.

✓ It can get **hot** in exam halls in summer: bring **a bottle of water** with you and don't dress too warmly! Note: if your bottle has a label on it, you will have to remove that before you can take it into exams.

✓ Bring a couple of black pens to the exam: you need to write in black ink and it is good to have **a spare pen** in case one runs out. Erasable pens and gel pens are not allowed.

✓ Bring pencils, a rubber and a ruler with you. Use a **ruler** for **straight lines** in diagrams.

✓ You can bring a calculator into an exam unless you are told you can't. However, you must clear anything stored in the calculator.

✓ You can't bring a pencil case into the exam unless it is see-through: a clear plastic bag is OK.

✓ Look at past papers for your exam subjects: the first page will list what you need to bring with you.

✓ You can't take any web-enabled device or device that can store data into the exam. This includes smartwatches as well as mobile phones, iPods, etc.

✓ **Do not talk** to anyone in the exam hall: it is strictly forbidden. If you need help from the invigilators, put your hand up.

✓ **Read** the front of the exam paper **carefully** and fill in all the boxes correctly. The invigilators will have the information you need for this.

✓ There will be a clock in the exam hall which will definitely be correct. Use it to **keep track of time** and **plan your answers**.

✓ Take some deep breaths before your exam to help you relax.

Many students have access arrangements for exams, such as scribes or readers. Talk to the person responsible for exams at your college or school about this.

113

Exam stress

The human stress response is something we have evolved as a species to power us through challenging situations. Stress helps us to perform at our optimal level – our brains work faster, our reactions are sharper.

Because stress is a natural response, it is not something we can decide to have or not have. But we can **manage** our stress.

Planning for stress

Plan time to rest and relax. This is as important as planning your revision sessions. Check back over your revision so far. Are you getting enough sleep? Are you breaking up revision sessions with time to relax? How are you enjoying your rewards – should you be rewarding yourself more?

Worry time

Sometimes it can feel like worries go round and round in your head. Health experts recommend actually setting time aside for worrying. What you do is this:

1 Set up worry time. This is a specific time of day when you will worry about things for a specific amount of time. You have to keep your worry time appointment each day for it to work.

2 Then, whenever you start to worry about something, jot down your worry. Say, 'I will worry about this during worry time'.

3 When it is worry time, go through the list of worries you've put together that day.

You can problem solve worries in worry time: work out ways to deal with them.

Some worries are hypothetical – 'what if?' sorts of worries. These are worries we can't solve and worrying about them won't be useful or helpful. These are worries we should try to let go.

Good luck in all your A Level exams!

Published by Pearson Education Limited, 80 Strand, London, WC2R ORL.

www.pearsonschoolsandfecolleges.co.uk

Text and illustrations © Pearson Education Ltd 2017
Typeset and illustrated by Kamae Design, Oxford
Produced by Out of House Publishing
Cover illustration by Eoin Coveney

The right of Rob Bircher to be identified as author of this work has been asserted by him in accordance with the
Copyright, Designs and Patents Act 1988.

First published 2017

20 19 18 17
10 9 8 7 6 5 4 3 2 1

British Library Cataloguing in Publication Data
A catalogue record for this book is available from the British Library

ISBN 978 1 292 19154 6

Printed in the UK by Ashford Colour Press

Note from the publisher

Pearson has robust editorial processes, including answer and fact checks, to ensure the accuracy of the content in
this publication, and every effort is made to ensure this publication is free of errors. We are, however, only human, and
occasionally errors do occur. Pearson is not liable for any misunderstandings that arise as a result of errors in this
publication, but it is our priority to ensure that the content is accurate. If you spot an error, please do contact us at
resourcescorrections@pearson.com so we can make sure it is corrected.